The Crowns, the King and the Long Lost Smile

A Play

David Foxton

A SAMUEL FRENCH ACTING EDITION

SAMUELFRENCH-LONDON.CO.UK
SAMUELFRENCH.COM

Copyright © 1980 by David J. Wood
All Rights Reserved

THE CROWNS, THE KING AND THE LONG LOST SMILE is fully protected under the copyright laws of the British Commonwealth, including Canada, the United States of America, and all other countries of the Copyright Union. All rights, including professional and amateur stage productions, recitation, lecturing, public reading, motion picture, radio broadcasting, television and the rights of translation into foreign languages are strictly reserved.

ISBN 978-0-573-05050-3

www.samuelfrench-london.co.uk

www.samuelfrench.com

FOR AMATEUR PRODUCTION ENQUIRIES

UNITED KINGDOM AND WORLD
EXCLUDING NORTH AMERICA
plays@SamuelFrench-London.co.uk
020 7255 4302/01

Each title is subject to availability from Samuel French,
depending upon country of performance.

CAUTION: Professional and amateur producers are hereby warned that THE CROWNS, THE KING AND THE LONG LOST SMILE is subject to a licensing fee. Publication of this play does not imply availability for performance. Both amateurs and professionals considering a production are strongly advised to apply to the appropriate agent before starting rehearsals, advertising, or booking a theatre. A licensing fee must be paid whether the title is presented for charity or gain and whether or not admission is charged.

The professional rights in this play are controlled by Samuel French Ltd, 52 Fitzroy Street, London, W1T 5JR.

No one shall make any changes in this title for the purpose of production. No part of this book may be reproduced, stored in a retrieval system, or transmitted in any form, by any means, now known or yet to be invented, including mechanical, electronic, photocopying, recording, videotaping, or otherwise, without the prior written permission of the publisher. No one shall upload this title, or part of this title, to any social media websites.

The right of David Foxton to be identified as author of this work has been asserted by him in accordance with Section 77 of the Copyright, Designs and Patents Act 1988

CHARACTERS

Thomas ⎤
Ben   ⎥ The Crown Troupe, *a strolling band of*
Will   ⎥ *entertainers*
Sally   ⎦
Little Girl
1st Citizen
2nd Citizen
Baron Wolframm Drax
Captain Hugo Enchmann
1st Soldier (Hans)
2nd Soldier (Kniell)
3rd Soldier (Engelbert)
Lady Philomena Wunderkind, *lady-in-waiting to the Princess*
Princess Dulcinea of Nostrovia
King Norbert the Ninth of Nostrovia
Archbishop Nuncillus
Townspeople, Attendants

ACT I

    SCENE 1 Approaching the Capital of Nostrovia
    SCENE 2 The Town Square

ACT II

    The Town Square

ACT III

    SCENE 1 Not far from the Capital of Nostrovia
    SCENE 2 The Cathedral of Saint Nostrum the Great

Time—a few whiles ago

PRODUCTION NOTE

The play can be easily staged in a few simple settings, which can be more elaborate as facilities permit. In the original production, an open stage was used, with two acting levels—a main upper one for the Town Square and Cathedral scenes, and a lower one for scenes taking place outside the Town, with access to the lower level through the audience. If two levels are not practicable, the play can easily be adapted to the available facilities.

If possible, the audience should be on three sides of the action to encourage participation when called for.

AUTHOR'S NOTE

The consideration of audience participation was very much part of the creation of this play. Participation should happen spontaneously though it can, and should be anticipated by playwright, director, and cast in that order. Participation is the outward demonstration of the audience's sharing of the play, it is a pointer to their involvement and absorption. The script has many opportunities for participation, they need to be discussed fully between cast and director so that "safety valves" may be built into anticipated vociferous areas and so that all possible responses and counter responses can be considered. The building up of relationships between the individual members of the cast and the audience is vital, and once responses are obtained they must not be ignored or shouted down, for in that way audiences are lost.

ACT I

Scene 1

The Kingdom of Nostrovia: approaching the Capital of Nostrovia. (See Production Note opposite)

Thomas enters from the back of the auditorium, banging a drum. He is followed by Ben and Will, who carry a large prop/costume hamper between them. They march down through the Audience

Thomas Come on, get a move on—we haven't got all day you know. (*He moves towards the lower acting area*)
Ben I wish we had. I'm tired out.
Thomas We must keep going.
Ben Can't we stay here?
Thomas Of course we can't stay here, we need to be closer to the town—now don't waste any more time. Come along . . . come along . . .
Will (*mimicking him*) Come along! Come along!
Ben He doesn't have all the luggage to carry.
Will That's very true.
Ben It's always us who have to do the hard work.
Will He never lifts a finger.
Ben Who does he think he is?
Will Who does he think he is?
Ben I said that . . .
Will Oh!
Thomas Come along—come along . . . this way.

Thomas marches into the lower acting area, banging the drum. Ben and Will follow closely behind him in step. Thomas stops suddenly, and the others bump into him

   Come on . . . come on. Over here you two.
Ben Here?

Ben and Will put down the hamper and sit on it

Thomas That's right. Now then this seems to be a suitable place to stop. We can make a camp here. The town's just over there—we can rehearse and be all ready for the parade in no time.
Ben Rehearse?
Will Parade?
Thomas Of course. As a strolling band of entertainers we must rehearse.
Ben But I'm hungry . . .
Will And I'm tired . . .

Thomas And I'm adamant.

Ben makes to shake hands, but Thomas slaps his hand away

No rehearsal means no performance; no performance means no money; and no money no food.

Ben \
Will } Oh! { *Together*

Thomas You may well say "oh!" Now come on—we'll rehearse the parade first of all.

Ben \
Will } *(groaning)* Ooh! { *Together*

Thomas Don't groan. Remember no rehearsal means . . .
Ben No performance.
Thomas And no performance means . . .
Will No money.
Thomas And no money means . . .

Ben \
Will } No food. { *Together*

Thomas Now then; the parade. I will go first, beating the drum. (*He beats the drum*) "Ladies and gentlemen, step up and see the world's finest entertainers. Today for your especial entertainment, for your amazement, you can see that world famous troupe of strolling players—the fantastic Crown Troupe!

Ben and Will begin to nod off

Never before have you heard such music, seen acts the like of which you can see today. For your delight, ladies and gentlemen—the Crown Troupe!"

He steps back to allow the parade to pass, but both Ben and Will are fast asleep

What's this? Hey you two—come on wake up! (*He nudges or kicks them*) On to your feet. Don't just lie there! Come on!

Ben and Will struggle to their feet

Ben Is breakfast ready?
Thomas I'll give you "Is breakfast ready?" Come on—jump to it—we haven't earned our breakfast yet. We must rehearse the parade . . . on your feet!
Will But we're tired.
Ben We could do with a rest.
Thomas I know . . . I know. But we'll rest later. *Rehearse* now—*rest* later. Now come on let's get organized. Now in the parade—I'll go first of course.
Ben Of course!
Will Of course!
Thomas And then you, Ben, and then you, Will, and then last of all will be . . . Where is she?

Act I, Scene 1

Ben and Will look around

Ben I thought she was following us.
Will She *was* following us.
Thomas Well then where is she now?
Ben I don't know.
Thomas Good heavens! I thought you were looking after her; if she's lost where can we get a replacement? There's nothing for it, we'll just have to go back and look for her. (*He puts the drum in the hamper*)
Will But what about the rehearsal?
Thomas We'll have to rehearse later.
Ben But I thought you said we were resting later.
Will You said we must *rehearse* now.
Thomas But that was before I knew she was missing. Oh don't confuse me . . . let's just go and find her. Now I'll go this way and you two can perhaps go over there and over there . . . and if you find her whistle—do you understand?
Will I can't whistle.
Thomas Well shout then, now let's all look . . .
Will What shall I shout?
Thomas Oh for goodness' sake—shout anything you like . . . Now let's go—don't waste any more time.

They begin to look, moving out of the acting area slightly, into the Audience

There is a terrible scream from the back of the auditorium, and the Little Girl runs down through the Audience, pursued by a bear, who is, in fact, Sally, the missing member of the Crown Troupe, dressed in a bear suit. The Little Girl runs across the lower level and off. Sally remains on the lower level, looking around. Will begins to move back on to the lower level with his back to Sally

Will Is anybody there? Yoo-hoo! Where are you?

He backs towards Sally, and finally bumps into her. He gingerly touches the fur, then smiles and turns round. He hugs her

(*Shouting*) Strawberry jam! Strawberry jam! Strawberry jam!

Thomas and Ben move back into the acting area

Thomas What are you doing?
Will I've found her.
Thomas But what's all this about strawberry jam?
Will Well you said I could shout what I like, and I like . . .
Thomas Strawberry jam! I understand. Now—(*To Sally*)—where've you been?
Sally Mmmm!
Thomas I said where've—oh take her head off you two, let her out.

Ben and Will remove the bear's head, to reveal Sally inside

Sally Whew! It is warm in there, thanks for letting me out, I needed some fresh air . . .

Thomas Where on earth have you been?
Ben We've been worried about you.
Thomas You will remember that I am responsible for you, when you joined our troupe you agreed to obey all our rules.
Sally Well yes I know but . . .
Thomas I told your father that I would look after you, didn't I?
Sally Yes you did but . . .
Thomas No "buts". You will recall that when you answered my advertisement for a dancing bear, I did explain that it was unusual to give the job to a girl dressed up as a bear.
Sally I know you did . . .
Thomas And I only took you on, on the understanding that you obeyed all our rules, and did the cooking, and the washing and your share of the carrying, and that you kept up with us and . . .

Sally starts to cry

Ben Now look what you've done.
Will You great bully, you're nothing more . . .
Ben Completely heartless you are.
Will Shouting at a poor bear like that.
Sally (*amid tears*) I'm not a bear . . .
Will Oh yes, sorry, I didn't mean it.
Ben You ought to be ashamed of yourself.
Thomas I didn't mean to shout . . .
Will Well tell her you're sorry then.

There is a pause

Ben Go on—tell her!
Thomas Hem . . . I . . . er . . . I . . . er . . . I'm sorry! There, are you satisfied?
Ben Thank you!
Will I should think so.
Ben (*to Sally*) Now . . . where have you been? What happened?
Will Blow your nose and tell us.
Sally Well. (*She blows her nose*) I joined the troupe as a dancing bear and he said that I had to keep up with you all.
Ben Yes.
Sally Well, I found I couldn't and the more I tried the hotter I became, and I couldn't get out of the suit by myself and I became hotter, and then you all walked so quickly that I couldn't catch up. And I got lost, so I stopped to ask the way to the town and I asked this girl who was collecting wild flowers, but as soon as she saw me she ran away screaming. And then you found me. And then he shouted at me. (*She cries again*)
Will Oh don't cry! You're safe now. And don't pay any attention to him, he always shouts a lot—he doesn't really mean it.
Ben It wouldn't be the same if he didn't shout.
Will We've got used to it.

Act I, Scene 1

Ben And you will in time.
Sally I don't think I ever will . . .
Will We'll help you . . .
Ben Yes, we'll help you.
Thomas Come on now! That's enough talking! Let's get on with our rehearsal. Now just gather round here and I'll explain the plan.

They group around Thomas

Tomorrow, after a good night's sleep, we'll parade into the town; all costumes and make-up on. I'll make the announcement about our performance and gather a crowd together while you set up the stage. It'll be a magnificent opportunity to play in front of a really good audience. You see this town is very rich and the people are very friendly. Yes, very friendly indeed. Once they're seen our show they will invite us back to their houses for meals, they're so very friendly.

Townspeople, including the Little Girl, begin to creep on to the lower level and surround Thomas and the others. They are armed with a variety of weapons, farm implements etc.

And we should find that we can make really good collections and then we'll be able to eat well for weeks and perhaps even find rooms at the inn. Who knows, we may stay here quite some time if the people really like us.

1st Citizen Don't move any of you.
2nd Citizen Stay right where you are.

The Townspeople close in on the Troupe, who stand and huddle together

Ben (*to Thomas*) I thought you said they were friendly.
Thomas That's what I'd heard . . .
1st Citizen Quiet there. No talking.
2nd Citizen Just stand still.

The Townspeople walk round the Troupe in silence

1st Citizen How long have you been here?
Will Not long . . . not long at all . . .
Ben Hardly any time really . . .
Thomas About half an hour.
2nd Citizen Have you see a wild bear around here while you've been here?
Ben A wild bear?
1st Citizen That's right. Not fifteen minutes ago my daughter was chased home by a wild bear, coming from this direction.
Will Oh that bear!
Ben That wild bear!

Will and Ben laugh

1st Citizen This is no laughing matter.
2nd Citizen It certainly isn't.

Ben and Will continue laughing

Thomas Let me explain . . . quiet you two.

Ben and Will stop laughing

    The wild bear as you call it is not at all wild. Indeed it's not even a bear.
1st Citizen Not a bear?
2nd Citizen Not wild?
Thomas Not at all. It is in fact one of our company—look here she is.

Sally comes forward

    Allow me to introduce our dancing bear—Sally. (*To the Little Girl*) Perhaps you'd like to shake her paw.

The Little Girl shakes Sally's paw

1st Citizen But what was she doing frightening my daughter?
Ben It was a mistake.
Will Not intended.
Sally I just meant to ask my way . . . I forgot about the bear suit until the girl ran away . . . I'm awfully sorry. I had the head on like this you see. (*She puts the head back on*)

The Little Girl screams again and hides behind her parent

1st Citizen It's all right dear. It's a pretend bear.
2nd Citizen Not wild at all.
Thomas Far from wild.

Sally blunders around until Ben and Will help her remove the head

    (*Taking advantage of having an audience*) And indeed, ladies and gentlemen, the bear is just one small part of our performance that will tomorrow grace your own market place. For on that day the Crown Troupe of strolling entertainers will give you a show that will thrill and amaze you, make you laugh and make you . . .
1st Citizen What was that?
Thomas What was what?
1st Citizen What did you say just then?
Thomas Er . . . ladies and gentlemen, the bear is just one small part . . .
2nd Citizen Not that bit.
1st Citizen No, the last part, the last part.
Thomas (*running quickly through his speech*) . . . Troupe of strolling entertainers will give you a show that will thrill and amaze you, make you laugh and . . .

The Townspeople begin to laugh uproariously

Thomas What have I said?
Ben That's amazing.
Will I never thought he was a funny man.
1st Citizen (*wiping his eyes*) Oh, are we pleased to see you.
2nd Citizen We are indeed.
Thomas To see us?

Act I, Scene 1   7

1st Citizen Yes that's right!
Thomas But why us?
2nd Citizen Because we need someone to make us laugh.
1st Citizen We need some really good entertainers.
Thomas Well . . . *here* we are!
2nd Citizen If you are as good as you say you are you will make your fortunes here.
Thomas (*to the others*) What did I tell you?
1st Citizen If you succeed you will receive many, many presents, and lots of money.
Thomas You see! You see!
Ben Ssh! Just a minute . . . (*To the Townspeople*) Excuse me . . .
1st Citizen Yes, what is it?
Ben Well, forgive my asking you . . . I . . . er, don't mean to be too curious, but I just happened to wonder . . .
2nd Citizen Yes?
Ben You said that if we are as good as *he* says we are, then we will make our fortunes . . .
2nd Citizen And it's true . . . all the money you'll ever need, all the riches and . . .
Ben Yes, thank you, I heard that bit, but what I want to know is . . .
Will What if we aren't so good?
Ben What if we don't make you laugh?
1st Citizen Then you'll be executed.
Ben Oh well, that's fair enough I just thought I'd ask . . . we'll be what?
2nd Citizen Executed.
Will ⎫ You don't mean it!
Sally ⎬ No! No! I'm too young to die! *Together*
Ben ⎭ So am I.
Thomas Quiet! Quiet! Quiet I said—let me handle this . . . Excuse me . . . I . . . er . . . that is we are prepared to put our show on for the whole town, but forgive me if I ask . . . how is it that if we don't please you, we will be . . . executed?
1st Citizen Oh it's not *us* you have to please.
2nd Citizen No! No! We'll enjoy your show no matter how bad it is.

Ben and Will respond visibly

Thomas Who have we to please then?
1st Citizen You mean you don't know?
2nd Citizen You haven't heard?
Thomas No!
Ben No!
Will No!
Sally No!
Thomas Tell us.
Ben Please!
Will Please!!
Sally Please!!!

1st Citizen It's a sad story really. This used to be a very happy country and a very happy town.
2nd Citizen All the people were friendly. All visitors used to be made welcome and would feel at home in no time at all.
1st Citizen Our King was good King Norbert the Ninth, one of the kindest, happiest, most generous monarchs you could ever meet. And everyone in our town, and in every part of the country was always happy and contented.
2nd Citizen Everyone enjoyed life.
1st Citizen And laughed a lot.
2nd Citizen Until one dreadful day three long years ago . . .
Thomas What happened then?
1st Citizen The King disappeared.
Thomas Disappeared?
2nd Citizen That's right, one day he was here, and the next day he was gone.
1st Citizen And he's never been seen or heard of since.
Thomas But didn't anyone look for him?
Will Didn't you organize a search for him?
1st Citizen Of course we did, we spent a whole year scouring the country, everywhere was searched, every building examined, every possible hiding-place was investigated.
2nd Citizen But no trace of him has ever been found.
1st Citizen He has vanished without trace.
Will How sad!
1st Citizen That's right! How sad it was, and how sad it *is*!
2nd Citizen And the King's daughter, the Princess Dulcinea, has not laughed or smiled since that dreadful day.
1st Citizen That's why we need you.
Ben To make the Princess smile again?
2nd Citizen That's it . . . yes.
Will And if we do . . .
1st Citizen You'll be the most popular people in the entire country.
Ben And if we don't succeed . . .?
2nd Citizen Then the Princess will remain sad and the Chamberlain, Baron Wolframm Drax, will have you imprisoned or executed.
Thomas That's a bit severe isn't it . . . I mean we can't help it if the Princess is not amused. . . .
1st Citizen The Princess will not marry until she can smile again, and she won't smile until she knows where her father is.
2nd Citizen Unless you can make her smile . . .
Thomas *Unless? Unless?* Of course we can do it—of course we can make her smile, we have entertained royalty everywhere, there is no-one who can fail to be amused by our . . .
Ben Excuse me . . . could we have a word with you please?
Thomas Pardon?
Ben Could we have a word please?

Ben, Thomas, Will and Sally move to one side

Act I, Scene 1

Thomas What's the matter now?
Ben We... we... don't quite share your opinion of our abilities, we—
Will —think we might not be able to do it...
Sally And I'm frightened...
Thomas Not do it? Frightened? Pull yourselves together. Artists of our quality can raise laughs never mind smiles. We've played in front of difficult audiences before.
Will We've never been executed before.
Ben And we'd rather not be this time.
Will We don't want our heads chopping off.
Ben We're attached to them!
Will And we don't want to hang.
Ben We couldn't stand the suspense.
Will It might kill us...
Sally And I'm frightened.
Thomas Frightened? A bear like you? Pull yourself together.
Ben No we won't!
Will We can't.

Sally begins to cry

Thomas All right! All right! We'll just have to make excuses... I'll talk to them while you pack up, and then we'll just go on our way as though nothing had happened. Will that suit you?

The others nod in agreement

(*To the Townspeople*) My colleagues and I have discussed your generous offer, and we feel that the terms of the engagement are not quite what we are looking for and therefore we would ask you to excuse us. Er... we have just recalled a most pressing appointment which necessitates our leaving straight away... er... now in fact... if not earlier... and I am certain that you will understand... besides we all have coughs... (*He coughs*)... and sneezes. (*He sneezes*)

Ben, Will and Sally cough and sneeze with Thomas, as they collect together their gear and begin to back off down the auditorium

Undoubtedly there is 'flu in the air, and we...

As they retreat, Baron Drax and his henchmen advance down on them from the back of the auditorium

Baron And where do you think you're going?
Thomas Er... well... we... we... we think it might be 'flu.
Ben We don't wish to spread the... er... germs.

Will coughs and Sally begins to cry. They move back on to the lower acting area with Thomas and Ben, and huddle together

The Baron and his henchmen climb on to the stage

Baron Are these the so-called entertainers?

1st Citizen Yes, My Lord!
Baron Who is their leader?
Thomas I am, Your Lordship.
Baron Then I command you and your company to make ready for an immediate performance. Upon hearing of your arrival I sent word to the Princess, she will be coming shortly to see the entertainment. Put your costumes and make-up on now. And you, townspeople, set up a stage for this band of unlikely entertainers. There is no time to be lost. Make everything ready now. I shall return with the Princess shortly. My men will ensure that you do not feel tempted to leave our fine country before you have given a performance, the performance, let us hope, of your lives.

The Baron exits

As Thomas, Ben, Will and Sally look at one other in horror, the Lights fade to a—

BLACK-OUT

SCENE 2

The Town Square

As the Lights come up, the Townspeople are assembling a makeshift "stage" (this can be simply a frame with curtains). Some of the Townspeople are setting up benches on both levels, and seats on the upper level for the Royal Party. Thomas, Sally, Ben and Will are on the lower level, grouped despondently around the hamper

Thomas Well come on then . . . let's get . . . er . . . ready. After all this will be our first Royal Command performance. (*He opens the hamper*)

They reluctantly prepare for the performance, putting on costumes and make-up, and arranging props

Ben It's also likely to be our last one.
Will Are we as bad as all that?
Ben Well it's not going to be easy to make the Princess smile, if it was someone would have done it by now.
Thomas Don't spend all your time talking, get a move on, we haven't long.
Will All right! All right! Keep your hair on.
Ben Never mind hair, let's concentrate on keeping our heads on!

Sally begins to cry

Thomas I wish that bear would pull herself together.

There is a pause, as they continue getting ready

Act I, Scene 2

Sally I didn't know it was going to be like this, I thought it would be fun and laughs all the time.
Will It will be if we're successful.
Ben And if we're not . . . ?
Thomas Let's not think about it.

After a pause, Sally begins to cry again

Will Now what?
Sally I can't *help* thinking about it!

There is a pause

Will Anyway perhaps we'll manage it . . . someone must be able to make her smile . . .
Ben I wonder what happened to the King?
Thomas He disappeared, the townspeople said . . . you remember.
Will No-one just disappears . . . vanishes without trace.
Ben I wish I could, right now!
Sally Perhaps the King was kidnapped.
Ben Kidnapped? You mean "Kingnapped"—hey that's not a bad joke —shall I put it in the act . . . ?
Will Only if you want us to be sure of losing our heads.

Sally cries. Pause

Thomas Come on! Come on! We mustn't be much longer . . .
Will Oh let 'em wait for us . . .
Ben We're being as quick as we can . . .
Thomas It's going to be hard enough to make her laugh without keeping her waiting into the bargain . . .
Ben She's not here yet . . .
Will Someone will tell us when they're ready.
Sally I'm nervous.
Will We're all nervous.
Ben Look at Thomas, you'd think he'd never done a show before.
Will He ought to be worrying about whether we'll ever do one again . . .

Sally cries

Ben Now you've done it . . . she's crying again. (*To Sally*) Come on . . . he doesn't mean to upset you . . .
Will I'm sorry, really I am.

The 2nd Citizen comes down to them

2nd Citizen Are you ready? The stage is all set up.
Thomas Yes we're ready—come on then, and let's really put our backs into it.

Thomas, Ben, Will and Sally move on to the upper level with the hamper and all their props etc. They disappear behind the "stage", taking the hamper etc. with them, ready for their performance

Most of the Townspeople move down into the lower acting area, to take their places as part of the audience; a few remain on the upper level

There is a fanfare and all the Townspeople stand, as the Royal Party—the Princess, Lady Philomena Wunderkind, the Baron and various attendants—enters and takes up its position to one side of the upper acting area

The Townspeople sit down, and after a pause, the Princess makes a sign to indicate that the performance may begin

Baron Let the performance begin!

The curtains open on the "stage" and Thomas walks on, beating a drum and waving on Ben, Will and Sally (who is wearing the full bear costume again) The procession walks off the "stage" and twice around the upper acting area. The audience applaud. Ben takes the drum from Thomas, as he goes back on to the "stage" with Will and Sally. The curtains drop, leaving Thomas out front. As Thomas speaks, one of the others beats the drum behind the curtain

Thomas Your Highness, My Lords, ladies and gentlemen (*Drum roll*) Today you are privileged to see (*drum roll*) the most amazing, spectacular performance (*drum roll*; I'm sure you will agree. (*Drum roll*) Today for your delight, before your very eyes (*drum roll*) will we, the most . . .

There are shouts from the Townspeople of "Get on with it!", "Come on!", "Don't waste our time!" etc.

Baron Quiet!

There is a drum roll from behind the curtain. Thomas shushes them. Everyone quietens down

Carry on.

Another drumroll—Thomas shushes them behind the curtain again

Thomas Thank you, My Lord. (*He rushes through his speech to discover where he was, and continues*) . . . the most outstanding band (*drum roll*) of strolling players in this land (*drum roll*) perform for you our finest show. (*He waits for the drum roll but nothing happens. As he looks through the curtains, the drum sounds*)

There is applause. Thomas goes off through the curtains. After a pause, the curtains open and the actual show begins. It should start with a dance of some sort for all of the Troupe eg. a Morris dance. This can be followed by other short turns (juggling, acrobatics etc.) depending on the abilities of the actors

Then comes the snake-charming routine. If possible, the last short turn should end with Ben left alone in front of the closed curtains. Thomas and Sally bring on the hamper, which now contains only the snake-charming items and Will, who is wearing a long sleeve on one arm to represent a snake. Sally disappears behind the curtains again

Act I, Scene 2

Thomas You there!
Ben looks round, miming "Me?"
    Yes you! Come here!
Ben looks round again, then sidles over to Thomas
    Quickly! Quickly!
Ben sidles more quickly, using a humorous move
    Now then. Are you trustworthy?
Ben mimes "Me?"
    Yes! Yes! *You!* Can I trust you?
Ben nods
    I want you to take care of this for me. (*He points to the hamper*) I'll be back in a minute! (*He starts to go off*)
Ben goes to touch the hamper
    I said take care of it, *not* look in it
Ben walks away unconcernedly
    Thomas goes off through the curtains
Ben moves towards the hamper again, and is about to look in
    Thomas comes quickly back on
    I said don't touch!
Ben jumps
    Thomas goes off again
Ben makes faces after him. He now begins to talk very quickly, almost in gibberish. The audience of Townspeople respond to him, and the real Audience should join in

Ben Who does he think he is? Leave it alone he says. I'll look in. Shall I? I'll look in? (*He looks into the hamper and takes out a turban*) Oooh! It's a shoe. (*He tries it on his foot*) No! No! It's a glove! (*He tries it on his hand*) No! What is it?
Audience A hat!
Ben A hat? No!
Audience Yes!
Ben You put it on your head?
Audience Yes!
Ben No!
Audience Yes!
Ben Ooooh! (*He puts it on his head and parades around the hamper, tripping over a non-existent stone. He takes a dressing gown out*) Ooh! That's nice! Ooh! That's lovely! (*He puts the dressing gown on*) Ooh yes! (*He parades round again. This time when he trips, he kicks the imaginary stone out of the way. He takes out a pipe from the hamper*)

14   The Crowns, the King and the Long Lost Smile

Look! Look! It's a pipe! I blow down it and the tune comes out here. (*He points to the end of the pipe*) Shall I try it?
Audience Yes!
Ben Shall I? (*He blows a short blast—very shrill. He puts his fingers in his ears*) That was loud, ooh! (*He parades around, tripping over the "removed" stone. He takes out a snake-charming basket*) Ooh look! It's a snake! It's a wiggle wiggle snake! (*He wiggles his arm*) It's a great big wiggle wiggle snake. I'll charm it with the pipe. (*He sits down cross-legged with the basket and pipe*) I'll try it now—the wiggle wiggle snake. (*He blows a tune—nothing happens*) Come on wiggle wiggle snake! (*He blows again—nothing happens. He peeps in the basket*) Come on wiggle wiggle snake! (*He blows a much longer tune*)

As Ben concentrates on the small basket, Will raises his arm with the "snake" sleeve out of the hamper and wiggles it about in a snake-like manner. The Audience respond as the "snake" disappears

What was it? A wiggle wiggle snake?
Audience Yes!
Ben No!
Audience *Yes!*

Ben blows again, and the "snake" appears. Audience response

Ben What's the matter? . . . A wiggle wiggle snake?
Audience Yes!
Ben (*pointing to the small basket*) In the basket?
Audience No!
Ben (*pointing to the hamper*) In the big basket?
Audience Yes!
Ben No!
Audience *Yes!*
Ben I'll look in here? (*He goes to the hamper*)
Audience Yes!
Ben I'll look . . . (*He opens the hamper*)

The "snake" appears and Ben screams. Will leaps out of the hamper and chases Ben around the stage, threatening him with the "snake". As they run around, Will shows the "snake" to the Audience, and then to the Princess. The Princess screams, and keeps on screaming. The audience of Townspeople freeze, as do Ben and Will. Thomas and Sally peep out through the curtains. Eventually, the Princess stops screaming, but begins to cry. Ben and Will walk backwards to the "stage", as Thomas and Sally duck back behind the curtains. The Baron rises

Baron Seize those players!

Some of the attendants seize the Troupe, who protest

Thomas	It was a mistake Your Honour!	
Ben	We didn't mean to do it.	*Together*
Will	It was a joke, Your Lordship.	

Act I, Scene 2

Sally cries

Thomas Be quiet you bear.
Sally I'm not a bear.
Thomas Well, don't cry like one.
Sally I can't help it!

The Princess, still crying, is led off by her attendants

The Baron steps forward to address the Troupe

Baron Well then: you were warned.
Thomas But Your Lordship, it was an accident, it . . .
Baron Quiet! You were told what would happen if you failed to make her majesty smile . . .
Ben (*lapsing into gibberish*) Ah, but it was the wiggle wiggle snake . . . (*In his normal voice*) I mean it was the snake that frightened her . . .
Will That's why she cried . . .
Ben She wasn't sad . . .
Baron Enough! I've heard *quite* enough. There is no excuse. You failed to make the princess smile, you must accept the punishment.
Thomas You mean . . . ?
Baron Execution!
Thomas But what about a trial? Yes, a trial—that's it—you can't execute people without trying them first to see if they are innocent or guilty.
Ben Yes—a trial—before a judge.
Will And a jury.
Thomas That must be the law.
Sally Please!
Baron A trial? (*He thinks*) Very well, you shall have a trial.

There is a sigh of relief from the prisoners

But no judge . . .

Gasps all round

. . . and no jury—I shall try you . . . and then we'll execute you!

Thomas
Will } But that's not fair! { *Together*
Ben

Sally cries

Baron *Silence!* And before the execution the townspeople deserve a little preliminary entertainment—so I'll see you sentenced to a day or two in the stocks. That will amuse them. Yes, that's a grand idea—most amusing—most amusing! Take them away to the courthouse and let the trial begin.

The prisoners are led away protesting as the Lights fade to a—

BLACK-OUT

ACT II

The Town Square

Stocks with four places are set up on the main acting area. A sack containing missiles (eg. bean bags) is lying nearby

> *As the Lights come up, the Townspeople come on talking noisily and surrounding Thomas, Ben, Will, Sally (who is crying) and their guards, Captain Hugo Enchmann and the 1st, 2nd and 3rd Soldiers. As the Soldiers put the Troupe in the stocks, they complain loudly*

Thomas You are making a grave mistake. It's a blatant case of injustice. I demand a lawyer, a council, a solicitor . . .

Ben It's all a very sad mistake. It wasn't anybody's fault really. You were there, you know. Give us a second chance.

Will We didn't mean it. It just happened. It's all part of our act, you see. We never realized that she might be upset by it.

Sally (*crying*) It wasn't me. I didn't want to do it. I'm not really with them anyway. Oh dear.

Hugo takes a hip-flask from his pocket and drinks from it

Hugo Come on. Take your punishment. Put your head in there. Chins up! ha! ha! Smile please. Don't look so miserable. And your hands go in there. Come on, do as you're told.

The Soldiers fasten them securely in the stocks

> *The Baron and his henchmen enter, and the Townspeople quieten*

Baron Quiet! Quiet there I say! So my friends, I trust you are comfortable —or are your collars just that little bit tight, eh?

The Soldiers laugh

What a fine picture you do make. Have you any complaints?

Thomas I'd just like to say, sir, that this is the most outrageous miscarriage of justice I have ever known. Our trial only lasted twenty minutes . . . it's a disgrace.

Ben He's right.

Will Outrageous!

Baron And what do you intend doing about it?

Thomas Well I . . . go on tell him.

Ben Well he's . . . you tell him.

Will He's . . . I don't know—(*To Sally*)—do you?

Sally I don't know, either: oh what can we do . . . (*She cries*) hoo . . . hoo.

Baron There's nothing you can do . . . and do stop crying . . . you remind me of the princess . . . do stop! Stop! I say.

Act II   17

Sally stops crying

(*Addressing the crowd*) And now my friends, take a long look at these criminals... have you ever seen a more unpleasant group of individuals? They are of course sentenced to death... and the execution will be carried out tomorrow... Until then they will remain in the stocks for you all to bombard. So come my friends... (*He points to the sack*) ... Here, throw something at them...

The Soldiers hand out missiles (bean bags), but the Townspeople are unwilling to throw

Come on my friends. Throw at them. Come on... throw at them I say... I *order* you to throw at them! Guards! Make them throw!

The Soldiers threaten the Townspeople, who throw reluctantly, and with very bad aim

Make them throw, I say! And make them throw straight... Do you hear me, Hugo?
Hugo Yes, My Lord!
Baron Well do it! See to it that they are thrown at! You understand?
Hugo Yes, My Lord! But how...?
Baron Do it, Hugo! Do it!

The Baron and his attendants exit

Hugo "Do it, Hugo!" It's always me... Come on throw you lot, who'll throw at the prisoners—who's going to throw a good straight shot! Come on now—that's an order!

The Townspeople begin to move off

I said that's an order! Come on and have a throw! Come back here! Guards, bring them back here!

The Soldiers round up the 1st and 2nd Citizens and bring them to Hugo

The rest of the Townspeople gradually sneak off during the next few speeches

That's more like it. Come on now, let's see you throw at the prisoners —you heard the Baron's instructions... here. (*He gives a missile to each one*) Now throw...

There is a pause while the Townspeople look at the missiles

Come on... throw... throw!
1st Citizen We don't know how to.
Hugo You what?
2nd Citizen We don't know how to throw.
Hugo What nonsense. Of course you know. Now don't make me very angry... just throw.
1st Citizen But we really don't know how to do it.
2nd Citizen Perhaps you could show us...

1st Citizen A little demonstration of how it should be done . . .
2nd Citizen And then we'd know how.
1st Citizen After all you are so very good.

There is a pause while Hugo considers

Hugo Oh . . . well then . . . if you really insist. Now look, the best way of throwing is to ensure that your balance is right and that you have room to really manoeuvre your arms. Just stand back and give me room would you. Now this is the stance . . . (*He demonstrates, and sways more than a little*) . . . And you select a missile—
1st Soldier Your feet are too wide apart.
Hugo —from those available . . . what did you say?
1st Soldier I just ventured the opinion, Captain, that your feet were slightly too wide apart . . . only slightly . . .
Hugo Well don't! Now you must always allow for any wind too . . . at the moment there's a slight breeze from the north-east so I should . . .
2nd Soldier North-west, Captain.
Hugo From the north-east, so I should ensure that my . . .
2nd Soldier He means the north-west.
Hugo I do not mean the north-west. If I'd meant the north-west I'd have said the north-west. But I meant the north-east so I said the north-east. And don't you argue with your superiors.
2nd Soldier But sir I was only trying to . . .
Hugo Make a fool out of me, that's what you were trying to do. Well I won't stand for it. (*To the 1st Soldier*) And that goes for you as well, when I'm going instructions I don't need advice do you hear! I am your superior officer, what I do is right, what I say is right. And make sure you understand it.

The 1st and 2nd Citizens begin to sneak off, watched by the 3rd Soldier

When I was in the ranks we daren't question our officers. To do so meant death . . . or worse. I remember those days . . . you men don't know how lucky you are . . .

The 3rd Soldier gestures for attention

And what's the matter with you?

The 1st and 2nd Citizens exit

3rd Soldier Sir! Sir! Sir!
Hugo Well? Well? Well?
3rd Soldier The townspeople, sir!
Hugo What about them you half-wit?
3rd Soldier They've gone, sir!
Hugo Gone! (*He looks round*) Gone!! You imbeciles, how did you let this happen? You'll be punished, mark my words! And so will they, they won't get away from me . . . I know where to find them, they'll be in the inn celebrating their escape with liquor, and joking about me among their friends. But they won't get away with it . . . I'll search them

Act II

out. I'll go now. You three remain here on guard and don't you dare let the prisoners out of your sight. I'll see you when I get back.

Hugo exits

The Soldiers sigh with relief

Ben He didn't seem very pleased.
Will Far from it I would say.
1st Soldier Quiet you prisoners!
Will He shouted at you a lot.
1st Soldier I said be quiet . . . or you might just be on the receiving end of my knife.
Will Oh!

Sally begins to cry

2nd Soldier And that goes for you too!
Thomas See here, you men, I don't think you realize your position in this business.
1st Soldier And I reckon you don't realize yours . . . One more word from any of you and you might just find execution beginning half a day early.

Sally sobs again

2nd Soldier And that means you too!

Lady Philomena Wunderkind enters, followed by a lady-in-waiting who carries a tray of food and tankards of wine. This lady-in-waiting is, in fact, Princess Dulcinea in disguise

1st Soldier Stand! Who goes there?
Lady Philomena Philomena, lady-in-waiting to the Princess Dulcinea.
1st Soldier Advance and be recognized.

Lady Philomena comes forward

Lady Philomena My goodness you are thorough. I never realized how good you guards were. I must tell the Baron, he will be pleased.
2nd Soldier Thank you, Your Ladyship.
Lady Philomena And where is brave Hugo, your officer?
2nd Soldier He . . . er . . . he . . .
1st Soldier He had some urgent business to attend to in the town. He will be back shortly.
Lady Philomena Well, in the meantime her highness has sent some food and drink to keep you company during the long duty. She is most concerned about your welfare and insists that you have only the best.

(*She takes the tray from the Princess and puts it down in front of the Soldiers*)

1st Soldier Well that's very kind of her highness.
2nd Soldier Very thoughtful.
3rd Soldier Mmmm!
Lady Philomena So drink up and eat up . . . don't waste a drop or a crumb . . . or a second.

The Soldiers fall upon the food and drink

1st Soldier Excellent vitals!
2nd Soldier Beautiful wine!
3rd Soldier Beautiful . . . (*He slumps to the ground*)
2nd Soldier He's had too much already, look—he's had too much alre—
(*He collapses*)
1st Soldier What did you say? Here what's the matter with you . . . what's in this wine . . . what's in it . . .? I feel all . . . (*He collapses*)
Lady Philomena "Sleepy" I think is the word you were looking for. It's worked splendidly, Your Majesty . . .
Princess I'm so pleased, we need all the luck we can get . . . Now release the prisoners.

Lady Philomena takes a bunch of keys from the 1st Soldier and unlocks the prisoners

Ben Ow! My neck's stiff!
Will Better than being hung though, isn't it!
Ben I don't remember, I've never actually been hung.
Thomas Be quiet you two. Help Sally out.

Ben and Will assist in releasing Sally

Thomas (*to the Princess*) And we must thank you for helping us to escape in this way . . . after this afternoon we thought our last day had come.
Ben It was all that blooming Princess's fault.
Will Screaming and crying like that.
Ben It wasn't our fault at all.
Will It was hers.
Lady Philomena Careful what you say . . .
Ben Why, you won't tell the Princess will you?
Lady Philomena No, I won't tell her . . .
Will (*to the Princess*) And you won't tell her will you?
Princess No, I won't say a word to her.
Ben Well there we are then . . .
Lady Philomena But the Princess will know all the same.
Will How can she?
Ben Yes how?
Lady Philomena Very easily really, you see . . .
Princess I am the Princess Dulcinea.
Ben What?
Will Oh no!
Thomas They've done it again!

Sally cries

Thomas Your Majesty . . . how can I explain. I'm sure my colleagues did not really mean what they said.
Ben It was a slip of the . . .
Will Tongue.

Act II

Ben Nothing more I assure you.
Will It was the heat of the . . .
Ben Moment.
Will That made us speak as we did.
Ben How can we ever . . .
Princess Apologize? Don't bother. I can understand perfectly how you feel.
Ben⎫
Will⎭ You can? { *Together*
Princess Yes indeed. Why else would I have organized your escape?
Thomas Why indeed?
Princess You see this afternoon when I watched your act, I really was entertained, and amused . . .
Ben⎫
Will⎭ You were? { *Together*

Sally stops crying

Thomas By us?
Princess Oh yes! I thought you all very entertaining and very amusing . . .
Thomas You did?
Ben But then why didn't you smile?
Will Why are we here then . . . ?
Princess Oh that's a long story . . . and we haven't much time, I don't know how long the guards will sleep for . . .
Lady Philomena Why don't we put them in the stocks, Your Majesty?
Princess That's a good idea, then you can hear the whole story.

They put the Soldiers in the stocks

Thomas There that's a job well done.
Ben I really enjoyed doing that.
Will I think the stocks really suit them.
Ben Quite a picture they make.
Will Wait till Hugo comes back. I'd like to see the look on his face.
Thomas Never mind about him now. Let's hear the story from the Princess . . .

They gather round the Princess

Princess It all began long years ago when my father, the King, disappeared. I swore then that until he was found I would never smile again, no matter how amused I was.
Lady Philomena From that time Baron Drax has tried many times and in many ways to make the Princess smile.
Princess You see I've also said that I will never marry until I smile again.
Lady Philomena And Baron Drax wants her to smile again, so that he can marry her.
Princess In fact he *will* marry me as soon as I smile again; he has said so many times.
Ben What, old sour puss?

Will Marry you, Your Majesty?
Sally You wouldn't marry him surely?
Princess What choice have I? The country is already in his control. As soon as I smile or laugh he will insist on the wedding taking place.
Ben That's enough to make anyone sad for centuries.
Will Fancy being married to a misery like him.
Sally What a terrible thing to happen.
Thomas Your Highness, now we understand. If only there was something we could do, some way in which we could help you.
Ben If only we could help . . .
Will In some way . . . however small.
Sally We'd love to help you.

As they speak, the Princess and Lady Philomena whisper together

Princess Well, as a matter of fact, there is a way you can help.
Thomas There is?
Ben Oh dear!
Will You're sure?
Princess Yes indeed . . . all you have to do is to find the King—my father.
Lady Philomena And then our worries would be over.
Thomas Very well . . . say no more, Your Highness . . . your word is our command . . . we will begin at once . . . if not sooner . . .
Ben Excuse me . . . could we have another word with you please?
Thomas Pardon?
Ben Could we have a word with you please?

Thomas, Ben, Will and Sally move to one side

Thomas What on earth is the matter now?
Ben We . . . we . . . don't quite share your opinion of our ability to help . . . we . . .
Will Think we might not be able to do it . . .
Sally And I'm frightened.
Ben You see we haven't a plan at all . . .
Thomas That's right, by heavens, we don't have a plan.
Lady Philomena But *we* have one.
Ben / **Will** } You do? { *Together*
Princess Oh yes, we have thought out a plan.
Ben I was afraid of that.

Will nudges Ben

Thomas What is the plan, Your Highness?
Princess Well if, as I suspect, Baron Drax is behind the disappearance of my father . . .
Thomas Yes?
Lady Philomena Well he won't have made a very good job of searching the country, will he?
Thomas No, that's a point.

Act II

Princess So what we need to do is to search again.
Ben What? The *whole* country?
Lady Philomena It's very small.
Will But we don't know what the King looks like.
Sally That's right we wouldn't recognize him if we were to find him.
Princess That's where our plan is needed.
Lady Philomena You see what we thought is that you could take the Princess with you . . .
Thomas With us? What a good idea—take you with us—an excellent idea!
Ben Wait a minute! Wait a minute! Don't you think she might be missed?
Lady Philomena Oh yes! We've thought of that.
Will You have?
Princess Yes . . . I'll change places with the bear—she can become princess for a few days and I'll be a bear. No one need ever know.
Thomas But won't the change be noticed?
Princess I think I'll make quite a good bear.
Thomas No . . . I mean won't our Sally be recognized as *not* being a princess.
Sally Oh! Now you're being unkind again!

She cries and is comforted by Ben and Will

Thomas Who me? Unkind? Surely not.
Princess Well it really wasn't a pleasant thing to say, was it?
Will Most unpleasant.
Ben And uncalled for—you ought to be ashamed of yourself!
Will Tell her you're sorry . . .

Pause—Thomas is unwilling

Princess I'm sure he is sorry, aren't you?

Thomas nods

So you see Sally—he didn't mean it. And after all just think how brave you'll be, going to the palace and pretending to be me . . . Not everyone would dare to do that would they?

Sally shakes her head

And yet you dare . . .

Pause. Sally nods

And Lady Philomena will be there to look after you.
Lady Philomena That's right, I'll keep you in the Princess's room, and if anyone asks I'll say that her majesty has a cold, and can't be seen at all. That will keep Sally away from the Baron, and everyone else, until you get back.
Thomas Well . . . it all sounds a bit risky to me.
Will And to me.
Ben And me.

Princess Risky? Not for you. Sally's the brave one . . . it should be easy for the rest of us.
Lady Philomena That's right. Come on! Where's your spirit of adventure? Go on Sally—you go and change with her majesty—I only hope her clothes fit you . . .
Princess I only hope the bear suit fits me!

The Princess and Sally exit

Lady Philomena And I think it would be a good idea if you, Thomas, came with Sally and I—then both of us can help her at the palace. Don't you agree?
Thomas Well yes . . . I agree. But I can't leave these two to cope with the search.
Lady Philomena Why not? I'm sure they'll manage very well—won't you boys?
Ben You can depend on us, Your Ladyship.
Will Show us the task and we'll tackle it.
Ben Regardless of danger.
Will Regardless of risk.
Ben Bravery is our middle name.
Will Trust us, Your Ladyship.

Hugo is heard singing off stage. Ben and Will quickly hide with cries of "Help, they're coming back", "It's the enemy!" etc.

Thomas What's that?
Lady Philomena It's Hugo—the Guard Officer—coming back.
Thomas What shall we do?
Lady Philomena You go and warn the Princess and Sally . . .

Thomas goes off

   . . . we'll deal with Hugo.

Ben and Will peer out from their hiding places

Ben ⎱ We will? ⎰ *Together*
Will ⎰   ⎱

Lady Philomena Just be ready when I give the word—that's all I'll need.

Hugo enters, rather drunk

Hugo (*singing*) "There is a tavern in the town
              In the town . . .
              And there my old friends sit 'em down
              Sit 'em down . . .
              And drink and drink and drink."
Whoops steady, Hugo, remember your position. Don't appear drunk in front of your men.
Lady Philomena Hello Captain Hugo!
Hugo Lady Philomena. How pleasant to see you. And what brings you here may I ask?

Act II 25

Lady Philomena To see you of course my dear Hugo, what else?
Hugo To see me? Oh my word! What can I say? In front of my men too?
Lady Philomena Aren't you pleased to see me, my little brave soldier?
Hugo What? Oh yes! My word yes! Er . . . just let me dismiss the guard, Your Ladyship, and then we can talk. (*He turns to the non-existent guard*) Guard! Guard! Dis-miss! (*He looks for them*) My word they've gone already. That was quick. What a smart body of men they really are.
Lady Philomena Can we talk now my Hugo?
Hugo I'll just check the prisoners, Your Ladyship—or may I call you Philadelphia?
Lady Philomena Philomena, Hugo.
Hugo Philomenahugo, what a lovely name. I'll check the prisoners my dear. (*He counts them*) One; two; three. (*He turns to her*) There that's done, my dear, four prisoners all present and . . . (*He pauses*) Wait a minute.
Lady Philomena Oh, how clever you are, Hugo; and how brave to guard . . .
Hugo Just a minute . . . I must count them again.

Ben moves into the empty place. Hugo turns to the stocks

One, two, three, four. (*He turns to Lady Philomena*) Four prisoners . . . or should it be three?

Ben gets out of the stocks

No, I'm sure it's four.

Ben gets back in

One, two, three, four. All present.

Lady Philomena picks up a tankard from the tray

Lady Philomena And here's a little surprise for you, Hugo, some wine I've brought especially for you—my own home-made elderberry—just for you. (*She offers him a tankard*)
Hugo For me? Oh no I couldn't possibly, already I've had just a teeny little more than I usually do.
Lady Philomena But you'll have a drink—for my sake? I made it specially for you
Hugo For me? Well . . . I ought not to, I am on duty after all.
Lady Philomena Please Hugo . . . please, for me!

Hugo takes the tankard from her

Hugo Well, just a sip then. (*He drinks*) One sip can't hurt anyone after all can it? One sip that's all—(*He drinks again*)—that's hardly anything at all. No-one can become drunk on just one sip can they? (*He drinks yet again*) My word this is strong, I feel . . . (*He stops, drops the tankard, goes rigid and sways about*)
Lady Philomena Help! Now!

Ben comes out of the stocks and Will from his hiding place to catch the swaying Hugo—he sways about for quite some time before they actually do catch him and put him in the stocks

Ben And now there really are four again.

Ben and Will shake hands

Will Well done, Your Ladyship.

Ben and Will hug Lady Philomena

Thomas, the Princess and Sally enter. Sally is now dressed as the Princess, and the Princess is wearing the bear costume

Lady Philomena Come on now there's no time to be lost. I don't know how long the guards will stay asleep. Sally, Thomas and I must get back to the palace before morning and anyone is missed or anything suspected.

Princess And we must begin our search.

They all shake hands and wish each other luck

Lady Philomena, Thomas and Sally exit

So come on now, Ben and Will.

Ben Coming, Your Highness. Come on, Will.

Will I was just thinking.

Ben What now?

Will Well it seems a pity to have these people in the stocks and not throw something at them.

Ben I see what you mean. Have we time, Your Highness?

Princess I don't see why not—I would rather like to have a throw myself.

Will What are we waiting for then?

Ben Only remember not to laugh, Your Highness.

Princess I'll try.

They arm themselves with missiles from the sack and throw them at the unfortunate Soldiers. They also encourage the immediate Audience to join in, and leave them hurling missiles at the stocks as they move off the stage and out through the auditorium

The Soldiers, with the exception of Hugo, begin to come round, which should make the throwing by the Audience more fun. As the Soldiers shout in protest, the Townspeople come on, laughing at the Soldiers' predicament. Gradually, they join in and eventually take back control from the Audience

The Baron enters; the Townspeople quieten and stop throwing

Baron What's all this noise? What's all this tumult?

Silence

Come on speak up you miserable peasants! What is it all about?

1st Citizen Please, Your Lordship . . .

Baron Well? Speak!

Act II

1st Citizen We're throwing at the prisoners, Baron.
2nd Citizen As you ordered us to do.
Baron What? Oh yes! Yes! Well carry on throwing, you're doing well.

The Townspeople resume throwing

In fact I'll throw one or two myself. Stand back and give me room. And give me something to throw.
1st Citizen (*handing him a missile*) Here you are, Baron Drax.
Baron Right then watch this!
1st Citizen Quiet please! Quiet! Silence for the Baron Drax who will now give a demonstration of throwing at the poor unfortunates in the stocks.

The "prisoners" protest

Quiet you dogs!
Baron Thank you. I'll throw now, watch this . . . (*He prepares to hurl a missile, but stops in mid-throw, staring at the "prisoners". He goes up to them, peering closely*) What's this?

The Townspeople begin to laugh

What is this? . . . Aren't you . . . aren't you . . . aren't you . . .? And isn't this . . . Hugo! By all that's precious someone will suffer for this (*He takes a bunch of keys from his belt. To the 2nd Citizen*) Here you! Release them! And the rest of you be silent. Silent! I said! Heads will roll for this! When I discover who is responsible I will deal with them severely. Stand where you are and be silent!

The 2nd Citizen releases the Soldiers and Hugo, who is incapable of standing up without his help

What does all this mean? Where are the prisoners? How did all this come about? Speak you worms!
1st Soldier Well, Your Lordship, it . . . er . . . we . . .
Baron Speak up man!
1st Soldier Well . . . I . . . I can't think straight, my mind seems fogged . . . there's nothing clear.
Baron What about you? What happened here?
2nd Soldier Baron . . . there was . . . there was . . . ooh! my poor head, I can't think . . . ooh!
Baron And what have you to say?
3rd Soldier Ooh my poor head!
Baron Your poor head! Don't think about your heads—you'll be lucky to keep them after this exhibition. Stand up straight when I'm talking to you. Heads up, feet together, and look smart. You're supposed to be soldiers. Name from the left . . . name!
1st Soldier Hans!
2nd Soldier Kneill!
3rd Soldier And . . .
Hugo (*singing*) Bumpsadaisy! I like a drink that is cool.
    Hands, knees and bumpsadaisy

> That is my own golden rule.
> Tara-ra-ra-raa!
> Hands...

Baron (*outraged*) Captain Enchmann!
Hugo (*attempting to stand to attention*) Here Baron!
Baron Can that be you?
Hugo (*inspecting himself closely*) I believe it is, Baron!
Baron What state are you in Captain?
Hugo Nostrovia, Baron—good old Nostrovia. (*He sings a snatch of the National Anthem*)
> Nostrovia! Nostrovia!
> The fairest state of all
> Nostrovia! Nostrovia!
> The fatherland...

Baron Quiet you fool! And stand still, don't sway about like that! By heavens someone will pay for tonight's misdemeanours. No-one makes fun of my guards in this way and lives to boast about it. I shall have my revenge on you all. Guards!

The Soldiers spring to attention, calling out their names as before

1st Soldier Hans.
2nd Soldier Kniell.
3rd Soldier And...

Hugo attempts to dance with the 2nd Citizen who is still holding him up

Hugo (*singing*) Bumpsadaisy! I like a drink that is cool.
> Hands, knees and bumpsadaisy...

Baron Quiet Hugo!

Hugo is silent

> Guards, just take me a few hostages here. (*He points to the 1st and 2nd Citizens and the Little Girl*) I'll have him and him and her, and escort them to the deepest cells of my castle. I'll hold these three hostages until someone returns my prisoners. Someone must know where they are, and as soon as I hear of their whereabouts the hostages will be released. I'll give you two days, and if you haven't found my prisoners in that time I shall throw the hostages to the wild animals. If you want your friends back—return my prisoners.

The Townspeople mutter amongst themselves

> Take the hostages away!

The Soldiers are about to lead them away when Lady Philomena enters

Lady Philomena What does all this mean Baron?
Baron Mean, Lady Philomena?
Lady Philomena Yes, Baron Drax, what does it mean? And what are you doing with these townspeople?
Baron It means, My Lady, that someone has engineered the escape of my

prisoners and until I have them returned I intend to hold these peasants hostage!
Lady Philomena But you cannot do that Baron Drax.
Baron Just you watch me, Lady Philomena!
Lady Philomena But it is illegal. It is against our laws!
Baron I am the law now in Nostrovia. My decisions are final!
Lady Philomena But what of the Princess?
Baron She will do as she is told. She will approve my actions.
Lady Philomena I doubt it very much.
Baron What? She dare do nothing else. Bring her here! Bring her here now!
Lady Philomena Oh! Oh! But I cannot!
Baron Cannot! Of course you can. I *insist* she comes now. (*To the 1st Soldier*) You guard—go and bring her to me now!
Lady Philomena But, Baron, the Princess has a cold, a very bad cold—she cannot leave her room!
Baron Nonsense! Absolute nonsense! Bring her quickly.

The 1st Soldier exits

And then we'll see her acknowledge my power in this country once and for all. I've been too gentle for too long with her, and her beloved subjects. But no longer, from now on this country will feel the might of Baron Drax, I will rule this country with an iron hand—with or without the approval of the Princess Dulcinea.
Lady Philomena I must protest, Baron, the Princess may well have gone to bed. It's late, and with a cold like hers I feel sure that an early night . . .

The 1st Soldier enters with the "Princess", that is, Sally in disguise. She wears a nightgown and cap, and holds a handkerchief to her face. Thomas hovers behind her

Lady Philomena rushes to Sally's side

Baron Your Majesty, pray forgive my disturbing you at this hour . . .

There is a pause

Sally (*in a muffled voice*) Don't mention it.
Baron (*looking at her suspiciously*) . . . But there is a matter of state that requires your urgent approval. I trust I may speak to you of it?
Sally (*after a pause*) Of course, my dear Baron.
Baron Your Highness, you don't sound to be yourself . . .

Sally turns away frantically

Lady Philomena She has a very heavy cold, Baron . . . you recall I mentioned it to you.
Baron Her voice does sound rather strained, I must admit. However . . . Your Highness, I must trouble you a little further; it has become necessary for me to take a few hostages in order to "persuade" the "criminals" who released my prisoners to return them. You do approve my actions I trust?

Lady Philomena It is against our law, Your Majesty.
Baron Come now, Your Highness, you and I *are* the law . . . you do approve don't you?
Lady Philomena Say "no" to him, Your Majesty.
Baron Quiet you fool! Your Highness, give me your approval now!

There is a pause: no reply

Very well! Gaurds!

The Soldiers spring to attention

1st Soldier Hans!
2nd Soldier Kniell!
3rd Soldier And . . .
Hugo (*singing*) Bumpsadaisy! I like a drink that is cool,
　　　　　　Hands, knees and bumpsadaisy
　　　　　　That is my own golden rule
　　　　　　Ta-ra-ra-ra-raa!
　　　　　　Hands, knees and bumpsadaisy . . . . . *etc.*

As he sings, Hugo dances with the Baron, and may well bump his daisy for him. The crowd laugh at his antics, and Sally cannot help but laugh with them. She instantly realizes her mistake, but it is too late. Everyone freezes in silence, and even Hugo sobers up

Baron Great merciful heavens, she laughed. She didn't smile, she actually laughed. Hugo—you did it! Great gallows, I thought it would never happen! Nothing can stand in my way now! Nothing! Tomorrow we will be married. Forget the hostages, forget the prisoners, forget the past! Tomorrow the Princess Dulcinea and I will be married. Today I am Baron Drax, tomorrow King Wolframm of Nostrovia.
Hugo Three cheers for King Wolframm!

Only the Soldiers cheer as they exit with Hugo and the Baron. Thomas and Lady Philomena lead Sally off, and the others follow quietly, stunned into silence, as the Lights fade to a—

BLACK-OUT

ACT III

Scene 1

Not far from the Capital of Nostrovia
The Princess, Ben and Will enter through the Audience on to the lower acting area

Ben We should have known it would be difficult.
Will I'm sure I said it would be.
Ben Well if you did you didn't speak loud enough.
Will What do you mean "didn't speak loud enough"?
Ben I mean *I* didn't hear you.
Will You never listen to what I say.
Ben What did you say?
Will You see what I mean.
Ben You spend your time mumbling, you should speak up . . .
Will I can't be responsible for your being deaf.
Ben Deaf? Who's deaf?
Will You are!
Ben What did you say?
Will I said "You are!"
Ben Now look here . . . (*He grabs hold of Will, as though to fight*)
Princess Oh please! Please! Stop arguing both of you.
Will } Who's arguing? { *Together*
Ben
Princess You are—both of you are. You seem to have done nothing but argue since we began our search.
Ben Well I wouldn't say that . . .
Will It can't be true . . .
Princess It *is* true, and you're not helping me a bit . . . how can we hope to find my father if all you do is argue all the time . . . ? I thought I could rely on you, depend on you . . . and all you've done is quarrel . . . it's not fair . . . (*She is about to be very annoyed*)
Ben Now look what you've done! Oh please don't be angry, Your Majesty . . . we'll not argue any more . . .
Will You see it's just that usually we both argue with Thomas but . . .
Ben He's at the palace so I suppose we were bound to end up arguing with—
Will —each other.
Ben } But it won't happen again. { *Together*
Will
Ben } I was going to say that. { *Together*
Will

Ben
Will } We assure you. { *Together*
Ben
Will } I was going to say that too. { *Together*
Ben So calm down, Your Majesty. We *will* find the King . . .
Will And in the meantime we'll try to cheer you up a little bit . . . Make yourself comfortable, Your Highness.

Ben and Will begin their "act"

A roll on the drums if you please . . .
Ben Pardon?
Will (*more loudly*) A roll on the drums if you please.
Ben All right . . . you don't have to shout. (*Shouting*) A roll on the drums if you please!

There is a pause

Will Well, do it then!
Ben Me?
Will Who else?
Ben Oh! (*He imitates a drum roll*) Brrmm . . .
Will Thank you!

Ben imitates a cymbal crash

Thank you again!

Ben imitates a triangle

That's quite enough . . . thank you.
Ben Don't mention it.
Will I won't.
Ben Please don't.
Will No I . . .
Ben I don't mean to trouble you . . .
Will Right, thank you, now . . .
Ben I was just doing my best.
Will I know that . . . thank you . . .
Ben That's all . . . just doing my best . . .
Will (*in Ben's ear*) Thank you!!

Ben jumps. As Will introduces the act, Ben imitates his actions

(*proudly*) Your Highness, My Lords, ladies and gentlemen . . . And now a special treat for you, that well-known sword-swallower . . .

Ben cannot follow all this

. . . Monsieur Cut-throat!

Ben looks round for this man

Come on! Come on!

Ben points to himself, miming "Who me?"

Act III, Scene 1   33

Yes, come on, come on . . . it's you!

Ben steps forward and takes a bow. Will claps

Ben (*aside to Will*) What do I do now?
Will Swallow a sword or two.
Ben Oh yes, thank you. (*He takes a pace forward, then pauses. Turning back to Will*) . . . I . . . er . . . haven't . . . er . . . I don't seem to have a sword with me.
Will Well then, swallow some glass or something.
Ben Glass?
Will Yes a couple of windows would do.
Ben But I don't want to swallow windows. (*Pause*) I'll get pains in my tummy.

They look to the Princess for a smile . . . but there's no smile: they look at each other and shrug

Will Well then . . . er . . . *you'll* have to do your escapologist trick.
Ben My what?
Will Your escapology . . .
Ben Oh! Well why didn't you say so . . . er . . . what does it mean?
Will (*to the Audience*) In this trick his hands will be fastened together, he'll be tied in a sack, locked in a trunk, and thrown in a lake.
Ben Oh! Is that all? . . . What! . . . er . . . excuse me.
Will Well?
Ben Don't you like me?
Will Get on with it! And remember you must remain under water for three minutes.
Ben Three minutes?
Will Yes, you must hold your breath.
Ben How can I hold anything if my hands are fastened together?
Will You fool, you'll have a knife in your pocket.
Ben I will?
Will Yes of course.
Ben Oh! I get the point.
Will But first of all I must blindfold you . . . keep still.

He takes a blindfold from his pocket and begins to blindfold Ben. The Princess begins to clap enthusiastically

Princess Oh yes! Yes! I like that! What a good idea!
Will I beg your pardon, Your Highness.
Princess I think it's a very good idea. Just the thing to cheer us all up . . . we'll have a game of Blindman's Buff!
Ben } Blindman's Buff! { *Together*
Will }
Princess That's right! Now I'll just fasten the blindfold on you, then Will and I will hide and you have to find us.
Ben Me?
Princess (*as she fixes the blindfold*) That's right . . . now can you see?

Will Yes!
Ben No!
Princess That's good. Now . . . I'll just turn you round three times . . . and you have to catch one of us and guess who you've caught . . .

She turns Ben round three times

One . . . two . . . three!
Ben Right! I'm coming . . . just keep still . . . I shall find you! . . . Over here perhaps . . . ah ha! . . . No! . . . Keep still . . .

Will and the Princess dodge round Ben, gradually moving away from the acting area into the Audience

Ben moves around, grabbing at fresh air, with of course, no success

. . . Where are you? . . . Ssh! ssh! . . . I'll hear them . . . Now . . . Here you are! . . . No! . . . Let me just . . . where? . . . Ah ha! Got you . . . No, not there again! . . . I'll never find them! . . . Come out, come out, wherever you are . . . *etc.*

The King enters, dressed in a gorilla suit and therefore unrecognizable. He watches Ben.

. . . Ah! Now there's someone there! . . . I can hear you . . .

The Gorilla dodges round the stage with Ben, joining in the game

. . . I'll get my hands on you in no time . . . Just you keep still . . . *etc.*

Ben grabs the Gorilla's hand

Ah ha! Ah ha! Got you! Now then let me think. Who is it?

He runs his hand over the Gorilla

Let me think . . . er . . . now who can it be? . . . It's . . . It's . . . it's you Will . . . I'd know that face anywhere . . . I've caught you! (*Taking off the blindfold*) Ah ha! (*He sees his capture*) Aah! . . . Ooh! . . . Help! Help! . . .

He tries to get away but the Gorilla pulls him back

Help! . . . Will . . . where are you? Oh help me!

Will and the Princess come back to the acting area

Well, don't just stand there . . . help me!
Will What can we do?
Ben Talk to him. Throw him a banana. Don't just stand there do something . . . help!
Princess We don't know what to do.
Will What do you suggest!
Ben Anything! . . . anything! Please . . . please, Your Majesty . . . Your Majesty . . . Your . . .

The Gorilla releases him

Thank you! (*He joins Will and the Princess*) Nasty vicious creature!
Will How about that!
Ben What do you mean?
Will Fancy just letting you go like that!
Ben Never mind that, come on let's run while we've a chance. Come on! (*He moves away*)

The Gorilla sits down

Come on you two!
Will No wait!
Ben What for? He might attack at any moment.
Princess He doesn't look vicious to me.
Will He looks sad . . . and lost!
Ben Lost! Sad! He's vicious I tell you . . . wait till he grabs you . . . he grabbed me didn't he? Don't go near him . . . come away!
Princess He looks as though he's crying!
Ben It's a trick . . . don't trust him . . . Come away from him.

Will and the Princess approach the Gorilla

Come back I tell you . . . he might sting you!
Will There!There! Old fellow . . . what's the matter?
Ben Just wait till he grabs you, then you'll know what the matter is!
Princess Are you sad?

The Gorilla nods

And lonely?

The Gorilla nods

Ben And he's hungry, so watch out!
Will (*patting the Gorilla*) Poor old chap.
Princess He's quite tame really . . .
Ben Don't you believe it. It's an old gorilla trick . . . he might pounce any minute!
Princess Don't be silly. (*She strokes the Gorilla's head*) . . . He's friendly . . . quite friendly . . . (*She shrieks*) OW!

The Gorilla stands up

Ben I told you! I told you! He's stung you!
Will What is it? What's the matter?
Princess I've pricked my finger . . . just as though it were a pin . . .
Will A pin . . .
Princess Yes.
Will On a gorilla . . . ?
Ben I said you couldn't trust him, didn't I?
Will (*looking closely at the Gorilla*) Just a minute! Just a minute!
Princess What's the matter? What is it?
Will Well, I may be wrong . . . but . . . now listen to me. (*To the Gorilla*) You're not a gorilla at all are you?

The Gorilla shakes his head

I thought as much . . . you're a man dressed up as a gorilla aren't you?

The Gorilla nods

Ben (*coming back to the others*) It's a trick I tell you . . . don't trust him!
Princess Well who are you really then?

The Gorilla mimes that he cannot talk or get out of the suit

Will What's the problem? Can't you get out of the suit?

The Gorilla shakes his head

Do you need help?

The Gorilla nods

Ben Be careful, Will . . . be careful . . . it might be . . .
Will A trick? Never! You know how we have to help Sally to get out of the bear suit. Here, come and give me a hand . . .
Ben I'm not sure . . .
Will Come on! It's all right I tell you . . .

Ben and Will and the Princess remove the head from the Gorilla to reveal the King inside

King Oh thank you! Thank you! At last!
Princess Father!!
King Dulcinea! Is it really you?
Princess Yes, Father. (*She runs to him and hugs him*)
King But why are you dressed like that?
Princess Oh it's a long story, Father . . . why are you dressed like that?
King This? Oh this is Baron Drax's idea. After he'd arranged my kidnapping he had me dressed in this suit. Without help I can't get out of it. So every day I've been dressed in this suit, and imprisoned every night. When I'm a gorilla the Baron feels free to let me roam the country for everyone I meet runs away from me.
Princess So that's why the search parties never found you.
King That's right. After all no-one cared to look too closely at a gorilla.
Ben So we've done it.
Will Done it?
Ben We've found the King. And the Princess can smile again.

Hand shakes and congratulations all round

Thomas rushes in

Thomas (*shouting*) Ben! Will! Your Majesty! Where are you? Where are you? Ben! Ben! Your Highness! Will! Are you there?
King Who's that?
Princess A friend!
Will Over here!

Act III, Scene 1

Ben This way!
Thomas (*breathlessly*) Oh thank heavens I've found you, I've been looking for you for hours . . .
Will What is it?
Princess What has happened.
Thomas The Princess has smiled.
Princess What!
Ben What do you mean . . . here's the Princess!
Thomas I mean Sally, as the Princess, has smiled—well laughed actually. And so the Baron is to marry her today!
Will Today? Marry Sally?
Thomas Thinking she's the Princess.
Princess And then he'll say he's the King.
King The blackguard!

Thomas jumps, suddenly noticing the King

Thomas Who's that?
Ben It's the King!
Thomas But why is he dressed as . . .
Will We'll explain later.
Ben We need a plan now.
Princess Before it's too late.
Thomas We'll have to move quickly for the preparations for the wedding have already begun.
Will Come on then, let's get back to the city.
Thomas And then what?
Will We'll make plans on the way.
Princess Come on, Father!
King Coming!

The King, the Princess, Thomas and Will rush off

Ben Yes, but . . . I mean . . . don't you think? . . . Won't it be a bit dangerous? . . . I said . . . (*He pauses*) . . . Wait for me!

He runs off after the others as the Lights fade to a—

BLACK-OUT

SCENE 2

The Cathedral of Saint Nostrum the Great

The Lights come up on the interior of the Cathedral. Parts of the town may also be seen in the background. There are flags everywhere and bells are ringing. Townspeople are standing about or sitting on benches on either side of the central altar, talking among themselves about the forthcoming event.

Thomas, Ben, Will and the real Princess mingle with the Congregation. Thomas and Ben are carrying bottles of wine concealed in their clothing

Hugo and the three Soldiers march on and take up their positions on one side. Archbishop Nuncillus enters, carrying the Sword of State and the Crown, which he places on the altar, before taking his place behind it. He raises his hand and the bells stop ringing

The Congregation stand and sing the National Anthem

All (*chorus*)   Nostrovia! Nostrovia!
The fairest state of all;
Nostrovia! Nostrovia!
The fatherland of all.

   1. A land of gleaming mountains,
Of cool and shining lakes,
Of rivers and of fountains,
And occasional earthquakes.
Chorus

   2. The tallest of the ice-caps
Is part of our fine lands;
The shores whereon the sea laps
Are made of purest sands.
Chorus

   3. The greatest of all forests
Grow strong upon our soil;
The houses where our heads rest
Were built with honest toil.
Chorus

   4. From north to south and eastwards
And far towards the west,
Our country marches forwards
The bravest and the best.
Chorus

As they sing, Baron Drax enters and stands in front of the altar. Sally, still disguised as the Princess, enters escorted by Lady Philomena. Sally is suitably hesitant and would retreat were it not for Lady Philomena. At last she reaches her position next to the Baron, as the National Anthem ends

The Congregation sit

Archbishop Dearly beloved brethren, we are gathered here today in this Cathedral of Saint Nostrum the Great to witness the marriage of these two noble people. Whereas the Princess, her royal highness Dulcinea Saskia, first daughter of King Norbert the Ninth of Nostrovia hath given her assent to . . .

Act III, Scene 2   39

Baron Get on with it! Get on with it!
Archbishop These matters cannot be rushed, Lord Baron . . .
Baron All right! But don't waste time . . .
Archbishop . . . hath given her assent to this marriage, it behoves me to address the Baron Wolframm Drax and advise him that at such a time as this all men are as one. The royal assent to this ceremony shall ensure that henceforward all shall regard as binding the pledges that will today be made. After this solemn service, this declaration of intent, it will be that the Baron Drax shall become King of Nostrovia and be crowned here in the Cathedral of Nostrum the Great, patron saint of Nostrovia.

The Congregation are not pleased. There is a slight moan, even a boo or two

Baron (*to the Congregation*) Quiet! Quiet! Or by the beard of Saint Nostrum you will suffer for it. Carry on bishop.
Archbishop *Arch*bishop.
Baron Not for much longer if you don't get on with it . . . get on with it!

As the Archbishop proceeds with his address, Thomas and Ben tempt Hugo and the Soldiers with wine. This should be done in full view of the Audience. Hugo and the Soldiers slip off stage with the bottles of wine, and Thomas, Ben, Will and the Princess take their places, holding the Soldiers' weapons

Archbishop To this end it falls to me to repeat the ancient laws of Nostrovia, first written by King Nirian in centuries gone by, amended by the noble King Nuncial of Nostrovia, revised by his highness King Nasrur the Mighty in the nineteenth year of his reign, reformed by his majesty King Norriman the Unready and re-written by his son, when King Norbert the First, rectified by the words of . . .
Baron Rubbish! To the ceremony! Get on with the wedding!
Archbishop But Baron it is tradition that these words be read, that the laws be . . .
Baron Rubbish! Soon *I* shall be law, I alone. Start the ceremony.
Archbishop Very well, since you insist . . . Dearly beloved we are gathered together . . .
Baron We've had that bit—get a move on!
Archbishop Yes! Yes, of course! (*Going quickly through the ceremony in his mind*) . . . er . . . in the face of this congregation . . . er . . . duly considering the causes . . . er . . . for which matrimony . . . First . . . it was ordained . . . er . . . er. Secondly it was ordained . . . er . . . er . . . Thirdly . . . er . . . both in prosperity and adversity . . . er . . . therefore if any man can show any just cause, why they may not lawfully be married, let him now speak, or else hereafter for ever hold his peace.

There is a pause

Thomas (*from his position as a soldier*) Yes, I can!

There is an intake of breath all round

Baron (*turning from the altar*) Who said that? (*Pause*) Who said that?
Ben He did!

Baron And who said that? Where is the scoundrel who speaks against me. Let him come forward now! I said, "Let him come forward now!"

The King, still in his gorilla suit, enters

The Congregation panic, climbing on the benches, screaming etc. The Archbishop hides behind the altar. Sally faints, and Lady Philomena tends to her

Baron (*slightly taken aback*) Do not be frightened, Your Highness, I will defend you against this creature, indeed I will slay it for you, in fact I'll take great pleasure in slaying it . . . Fear not, my own Princess. (*He bends down over Sally*) Fear not, my own Princess, I . . . (*He pauses*) . . . What's this? (*Furiously*) Great gallows, who is this?

Sally comes to

You are not the Princess . . . Guards! Seize this imposter!

Nothing happens

Guards, I said seize this imposter . . .

Still nothing

Are you all deaf? (*He moves towards the "guards"*) I said . . . I ordered you to seize this imposter . . . I . . . (*He moves rapidly from one to the other*) What on earth? More imposters . . . by the beard of Nostrum the Great . . . is anyone real? . . . Help me! . . . Captain Enchmann! . . . Hugo! . . . Help me!

Hugo stumbles on, drunk and clutching the now empty wine bottle

Hugo (*singing*) Hands, knees, and bumpsadaisy
                I like a drink that is cool!
                Hands, knees and bumpsadaisy . . .

Baron You oaf—you buffoon—is there no-one here I can rely on, is there no real member of the Court here?

Thomas and the others help to remove the gorilla head from the King

King I am real, Baron Drax.

All (*variously*) It's the King. Norbert the Ninth. His majesty the King. The King's back. He's returned. Thank heavens. Our King. A real King again . . . etc.

Baron Will nothing ever work out for me? I should have cut you down as soon as you made your appearance.

Thomas, Ben and Will move in on the Baron

Back you peasants. You'll not beat me as easily as this; all I have to do is to run his majesty through and once again I shall be in command. (*He turns to the King, drawing his sword*)

Lady Philomena hands the King the Sword of State from the altar

Lady Philomena Here you are, Your Majesty.

Act III, Scene 2   41

King Many thanks, Lady Philomena.

The King and the Baron fight. The Baron tries many dirty tricks, but is finally driven to his knees, begging for mercy

Baron Mercy! Mercy! Your Majesty, do not take my life; show mercy, Your Royal Highness, I beg you.

There is a pause

King Very well, Drax, you have your life. I will be merciful. (*He turns to the Congregation*) And now most devoted subjects . . .

The Baron draws a dagger and goes to stab the King; all shout out warnings, but before the King can turn around, Hugo knocks out the Baron with his bottle. There are cheers all round

Thank you Captain Enchmann.

Hugo salutes and collapses

I see you have changed little during my years of absence.

Everyone laughs

Look after him someone.

Lady Philomena and the Archbishop attend to Hugo

And take Baron Drax down to our deepest dungeon, I'll consider what to do with him later, much later . . . in fact someone might remind me . . . in about ten years!

More laughter. Some of the Townspeople drag the Baron off stage

And now there's little that remains to be done but to thank you four for your efforts—without you I would still be confined to a gorilla suit, my daughter would be married to Baron Drax and Nostrovia would be ruled by a tyrant. How can I thank you enough? What can I offer you as a reward?

Ben, Will and Sally think together

Ben Well . . . er . . .
Will Perhaps . . . er . . .
Sally Er . . .
Thomas Your Majesty, you owe us nothing. It has been our pleasure, our delight to be here and to help in any way we can, I know I am speaking for my colleagues when I say . . .
Ben Excuse me . . . could we have yet another word with you please?
Thomas Pardon?
Ben Could we have a word with you please!
Thomas (*to the King*) Excuse me.

Thomas, Ben, Will and Sally group together

What on earth is the matter now?

Will We thought we should ask for . . .
Ben Money or perhaps a little estate somewhere.
Will You see, we think we deserve it.
Sally And I don't want to go back to being a bear again . . .
Thomas Don't be silly, pull yourselves together. Don't you understand, we can't ask these kind people to give . . .
Will Oh yes we can!

The King, The Princess and the Townspeople are listening to them

Thomas We were only doing a service, we don't really want a reward.
Ben ⎫
Sally ⎭ Oh yes we do. { *Together*
Thomas You don't mean to say that they will give us a reward and perhaps a permanent job as court entertainers.
Ben ⎫
Will ⎬ Oh yes they will! { *Together*
Sally ⎭
Thomas Oh no they won't!
All Oh yes they will!!!

The Crowns jump

King There you see, Thomas—you were wrong. We are so grateful to you that from here on you are appointed Court Entertainers to his majesty King Norbert the Ninth of Nostrovia. You need never more worry about your future. What do you say; do you accept?
Thomas What do *we* say?
Princess Yes, what do you say?
Thomas ⎫   Nostrovia! Nostrovia!
Will   ⎬ *(singing)* What more can we four say, ⎫ *Together*
Ben   ⎪   Nostrovia! Nostrovia!   ⎭
Sally ⎭   The Crowns are here to stay!

Everyone cheers

All *(singing as they exit)*
        From north to south and eastwards,
        And far towards the west,
        Our country marches forwards
        The bravest and the best!

        Nostrovia! Nostrovia!
        This fairest state we call
        Nostrovia! Nostrovia!
        The fatherland of all.

The Lights fade to a—

BLACK-OUT

FURNITURE AND PROPERTY LIST

ACT I

Scene 1

Off stage: Drum **(Thomas)**
Hamper. *In it:* costumes, props, make-up, mirrors, turban, dressing gown, pipe, small basket, "snake" sleeve (*all items needed for Scene 2*) **(Ben and Will)**
Weapons and farm implements **(Townspeople)**

Personal: Sally: handkerchief

Scene 2

Set: Materials for makeshift "stage"
Benches
Seats

ACT II

Strike: Makeshift "stage"
Benches
Seats
Hamper and contents

Set: Stocks for 4 people
Sack of missiles (eg. bean bags)

Off stage: Tray. *On it:* food and tankards of wine **(Princess)**

Personal: Hugo: hip-flask
Soldiers: weapons
1st Soldier: bunch of keys
Baron: bunch of keys
Sally: handkerchief

ACT III

Scene 1

Strike: Stocks
Sack and missiles
Tray and tankards

Personal: Will: blindfold

SCENE 2

Set: Altar
Benches
Flags

Off stage: Sword of State **(Archbishop)**
Crown **(Archbishop)**
Bottle of wine **(Thomas)**
Bottle of wine **(Ben)**
Empty bottle **(Hugo)**

Personal: **Soldiers:** weapons
Baron: sword and dagger

LIGHTING PLOT

The following plot may be elaborated according to the facilities available eg. follow spots on characters as they enter or exit through the audience
Property fittings required: nil
Various exterior settings; one interior setting

ACT I, SCENE 1
To open: General lighting on lower acting area
Cue 1   **Baron** exits   (Page 10)
         Fade to Black-out

ACT 1, SCENE 2
To open: General lighting on both acting areas
Cue 2   **Thomas, Ben, Will** and **Sally** are led off   (Page 15)
         Fade to Black-out

ACT II
To open: General lighting on both acting areas
Cue 3   General movement off stage   (Page 30)
         Fade to Black-out

ACT III, SCENE 1
To open: General lighting on lower acting area
Cue 4   **Ben** runs off stage   (Page 37)
         Fade to Black-out

ACT III, SCENE 2
To open: General lighting for Cathedral
Cue 5   Cast move off stage, singing   (Page 42)
         Fade to Black-out

EFFECTS PLOT

ACT I
Scene 1

No cues

ACT I
Scene 2

Cue 1	Townspeople move down stage to take their seats *Fanfare*	(Page 12)

ACT II

No cues

ACT III
Scene 2

Cue 2	As Lights come up *Bells ring*	(Page 37)
Cue 3	**Archbishop** raises his hand *Bells stop ringing*	(Page 38)

www.ingramcontent.com/pod-product-compliance
Ingram Content Group UK Ltd
Pitfield, Milton Keynes, MK11 3LW, UK
UKHW021848210426
5322IPUK00022B/539